Fantastic Fashion Origami

Hats and Accessories

PowerKiDS press.

CATHERINE ARD

Published in 2020 by **The Rosen Publishing Group, Inc.**
29 East 21st Street, New York, NY 10010

Cataloging-in-Publication Data

Names: Ard, Catherine.
Title: Hats and accessories / Catherine Ard.
Description: New York : PowerKids Press, 2020. | Series: Fantastic fashion origami | Includes glossary and index.
Identifiers: ISBN 9781725302860 (pbk.) | ISBN 9781725302884 (library bound) | ISBN 9781725302877 (6 pack)
Subjects: LCSH: Origami--Juvenile literature. | Paper work--Juvenile literature. | Fashion--Juvenile literature. | Dress accessories--Juvenile literature.
Classification: LCC TT872.5 A73 2019 | DDC 736.982--dc23

Models and photography by Michael Wiles
Written by Catherine Ard
Designed by Picnic
Edited by Kate Overy and Joe Fullman

Manufactured in the United States of America

CPSIA Compliance Information: Batch CSPK19: For Further Information contact Rosen Publishing, New York, New York at 1-800-237-9932.

Contents

Introduction

This book shows you how to create a gorgeous collection of mini fashions. All you need for each item is a square of paper, your fingers, and some clever creasing. So, forget sewing and get folding!

Getting started

The paper used in origami is thin, but strong, so that it can be folded many times. You can use ordinary scrap paper, but make sure it's not too thick.

A lot of the clothes in this book are made with the same folds. The ones that appear most are explained on these pages. It's a good idea to master these folds before you start.

Key

When making your fashions, follow this key to find out what the lines, arrows, and symbols mean.

mountain fold ....

valley fold - - - - - - - - - - - - -

direction to move paper ↷

direction to push or pull paper ▶

hold paper in place with finger ☛

Mountain fold

To make a mountain fold, fold the paper so that the crease is pointing up at you, like a mountain.

Valley fold

To make a valley fold, fold the paper the other way, so that the crease is pointing away from you, like a valley.

Sunglasses

Keep your cool with these designer sunglasses. It only takes a few easy folds and a lot of rolls to create these trendy wraparound shades.

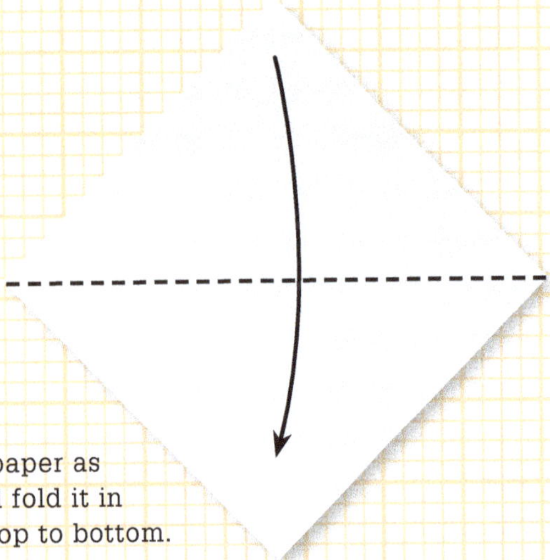

1

Place the paper as shown and fold it in half from top to bottom.

2

Taking the top layer only, fold in the tip of the bottom corner around ¾ inch (19 mm) from the point.

3

Make a crease around ½ inch (13 mm) from the top edge. Fold the paper over, keeping it straight.

4

Roll the paper over, creasing the paper next to the fold you just made.

5

Roll and crease the paper again in the same way. Press down firmly after each roll.

Easy

6 Make a total of five folds in this way to create a thin band of paper. This will become the arms of the sunglasses.

7 Make a mountain fold at the bottom around ¼ inch (6 mm) from the bottom of the top layer.

8 Shape the arms with a mountain fold at either end, alongside the first diagonal stripe.

9 Make two final mountain folds on either side, as shown, to transform the paper into a pair of sunglasses.

10 Your cool shades are ready for bright summer days. Bring on the sunshine!

Bangle

Get ready to roll a fab bangle without the jingling and jangling. Choose a bright paper to create really dazzling diagonal stripes.

1

Place the paper as shown. Fold it in half from top to bottom and unfold, then from left to right and unfold.

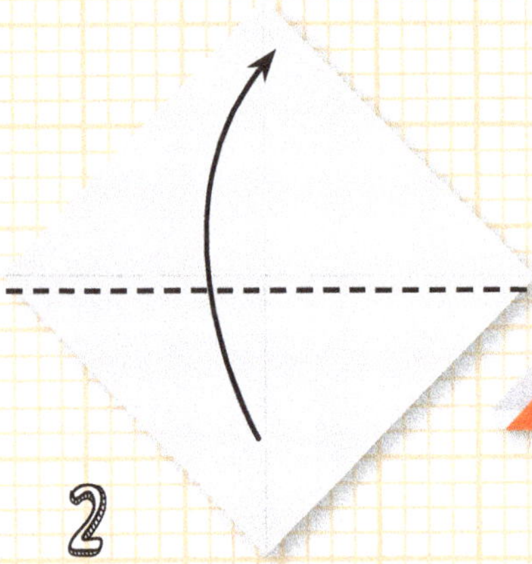

2

Valley fold the paper from bottom to top, leaving a ¼-inch (6 mm) border of white around the top edges.

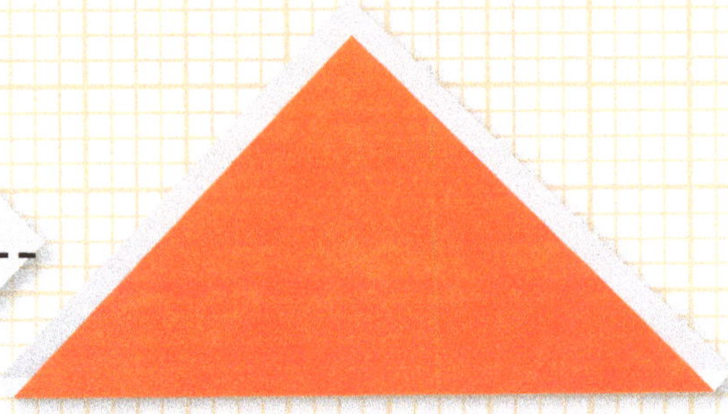

3

Turn the paper over.

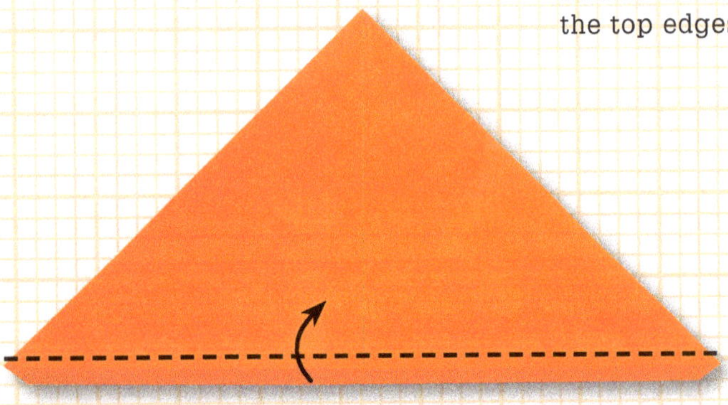

4 Fold the bottom edge in with a valley fold ¼ inch (6 mm) above the central crease.

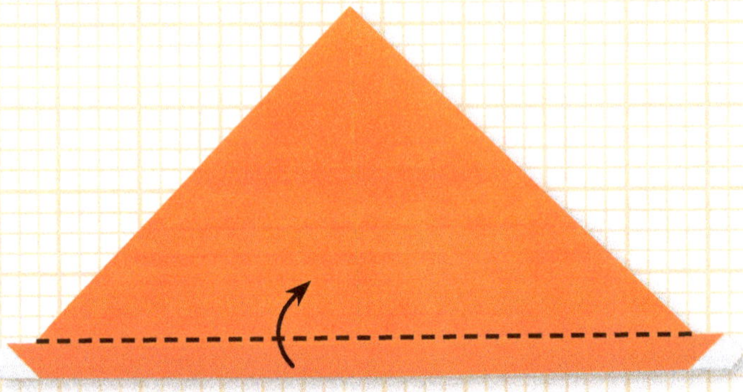

5 Roll the paper over, creasing the paper next to the fold you just made.

6

Roll over and crease again. You can see the pattern of diagonal stripes beginning to appear at either end.

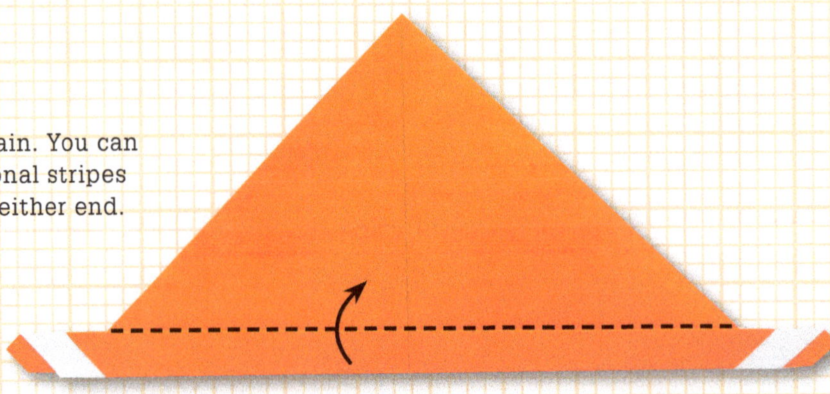

Easy

7

Continue to roll and crease the paper in the same way, pressing down firmly after each roll.

8 When all of the paper is rolled into a band, secure the point with a piece of sticky tape. Bend the ends around and bring them together in a circle. Slide one end between the folds on the other end to hold it in place.

9

Your stripy bangle is finished. You can fold an armful of paper bling that hardly costs a thing!

Socks

Don't worry about odd socks on paper laundry day. Fold lots of pairs, pin them on a clothesline, and watch them flutter in the breeze for fun!

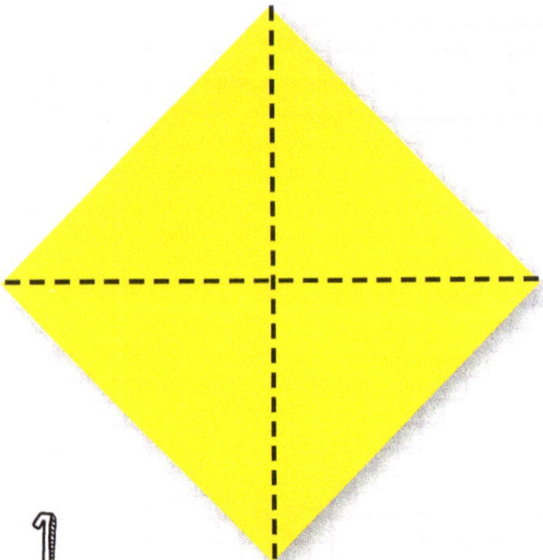

1

Place the paper as shown. Fold it in half from top to bottom and unfold, then from left to right and unfold.

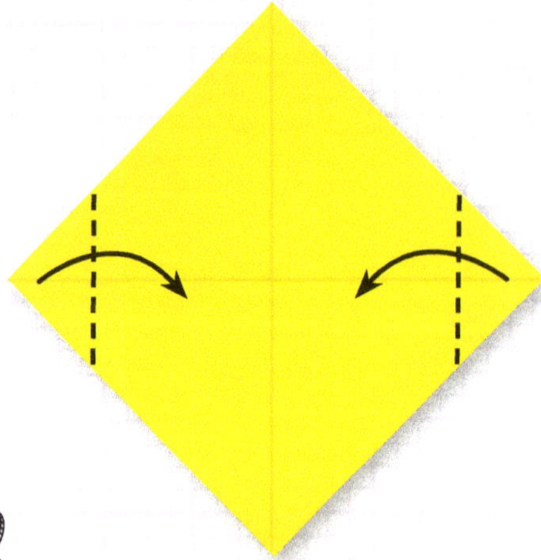

2

Make creases on either side, 1¾ inches (44 mm) from the points, and fold in the corners.

3

Turn the paper over.

4

Make a crease at the bottom corner around 1½ inches (38 mm) from the point and fold in.

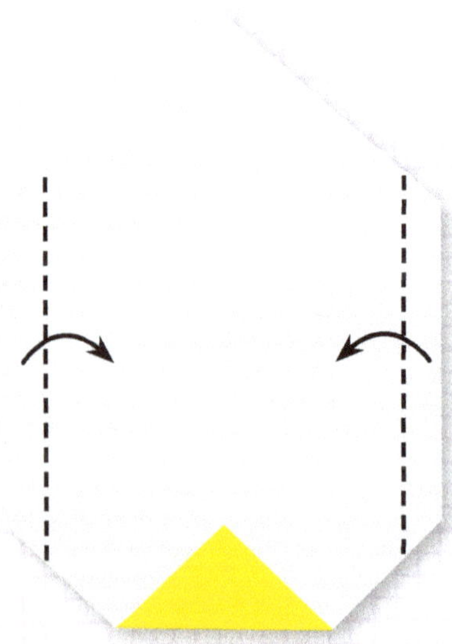

5

Valley fold a ¾-inch (19mm) section on the left and right edges. Make sure the creases are straight.

6

Make a new crease across the top as shown and fold down the corner.

★ ★ Medium

7 Turn the paper over.

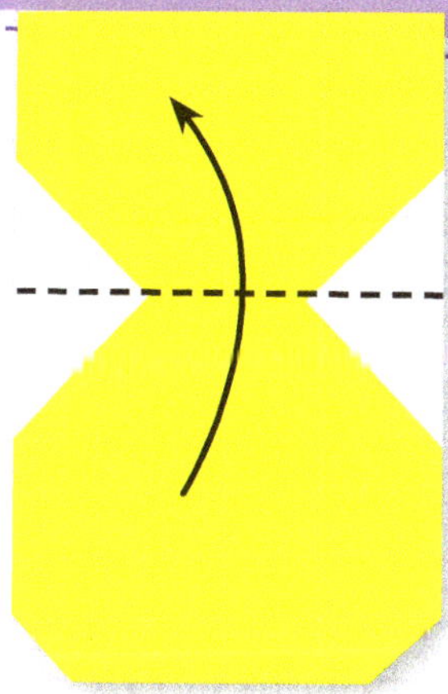

8 Fold the paper in half from bottom to top along the central crease.

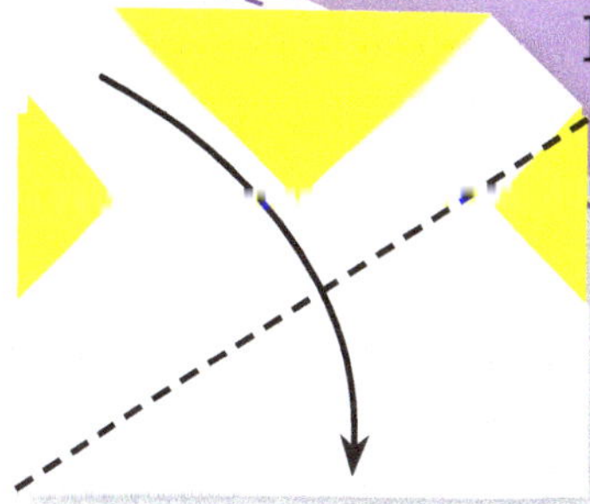

9 Taking the top layer only, fold the paper in half diagonally from top to bottom as shown.

10 Look carefully and you will see creases across the paper that you made earlier. Mountain fold along these creases.

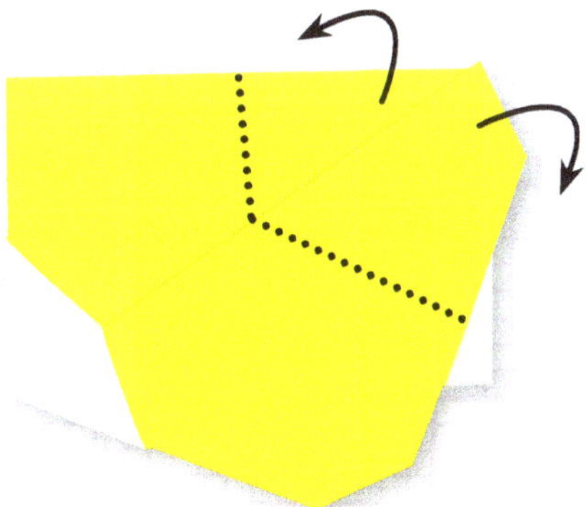

11 Fold back the top section first to make the upper part of the sock. Then fold down the bottom section, pressing down as shown to make the foot shape.

12 Shape the toe with a mountain fold on the corner.

13 Your sock is finished. Now fold another sock to make a perfect pair.

Boots

Footwear doesn't need to be black or brown. Be bold with red, yellow, or blue, and fold some trendy heeled boots topped with a white trim.

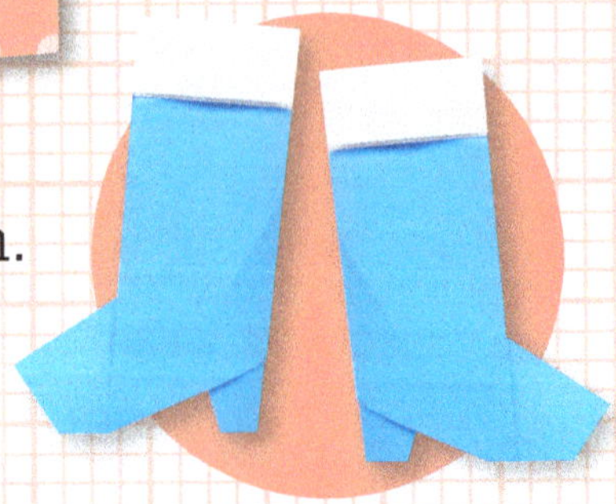

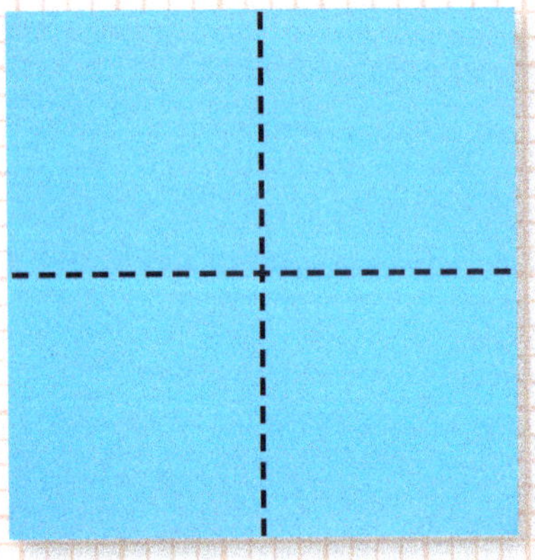

1 Fold the paper from left to right and unfold, then from top to bottom and unfold.

2 Make a crease about 1 inch (25 mm) from the top edge and fold the paper over.

3 Turn the paper over.

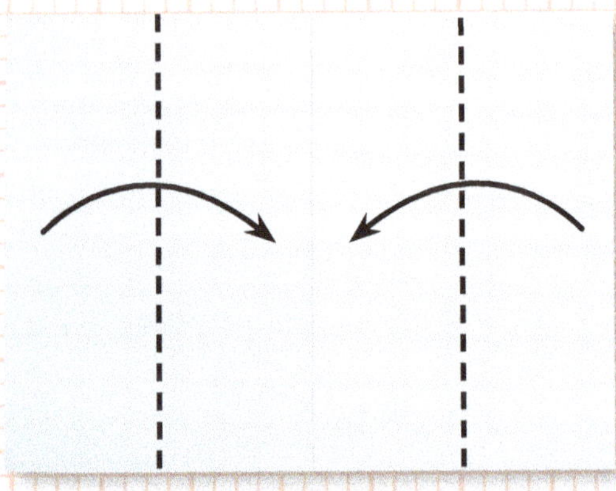

4 Fold the left and right edges in to meet the central crease.

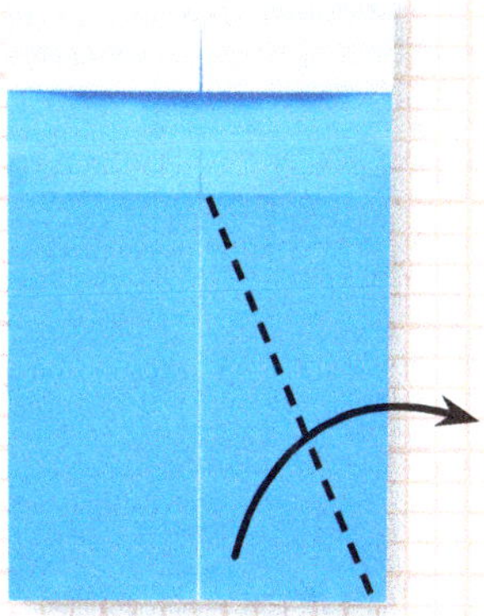

5 On the top layer, make a crease from the middle point to the bottom right corner.

6 Fold the paper over along the crease. Now unfold the left-hand side.

7 Valley fold the paper from the central crease on the left edge to the right edge as shown.

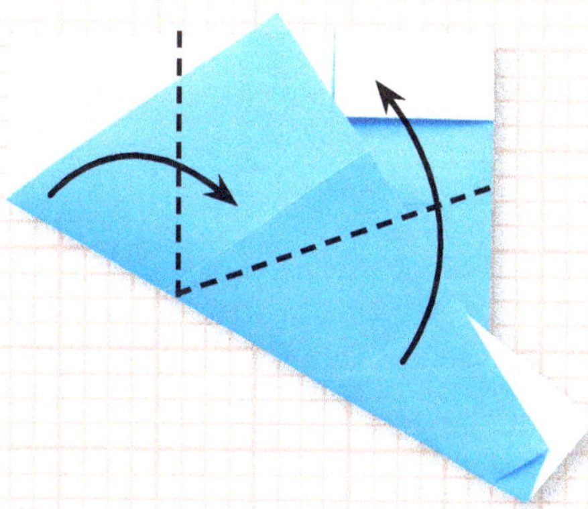

8 Fold over the left side along the crease you made in step 4. Make a diagonal fold from the bottom of this crease to the right edge, just above the central crease, then unfold.

9

Take the top corner and fold it down along the crease you just made.

10 Fold the left edge over to meet the middle and press the paper flat.

11 Valley fold the tip of the white corner as shown, then fold the paper in half from right to left.

12

Tuck the white band on the right inside the band on the left to secure it.

★★ Medium

13

Your boot is nearly finished. Mountain fold the tip of the bottom corner to make the sole.

14

Your boot is now ready. To create a pair, follow the same steps, but make all the folds on the opposite side.

Mittens

It takes some clever folding to create a pair of cozy mittens. Make a beanie hat to match the mittens and you are all ready for a paper snowball fight!

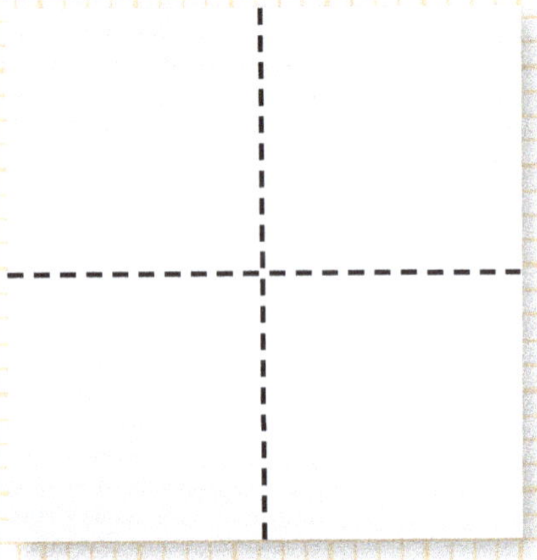

1 Fold the paper in half from top to bottom and unfold. Then fold it from left to right and unfold.

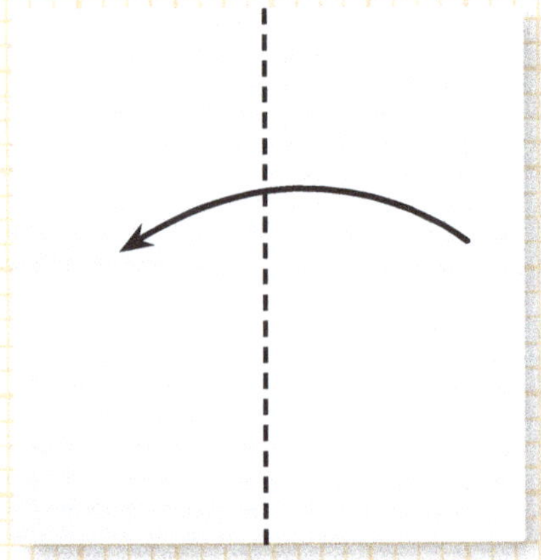

2 Fold the paper in half again from right to left.

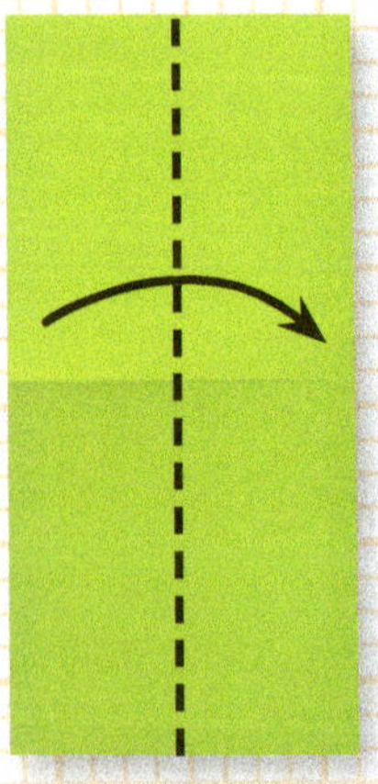

3 Taking the top layer only, fold the left edge over to meet the right edge.

4 Make a diagonal crease from the bottom corner as shown. Make another crease that meets it in a V, then unfold both creases.

★ ★ ★

Hard

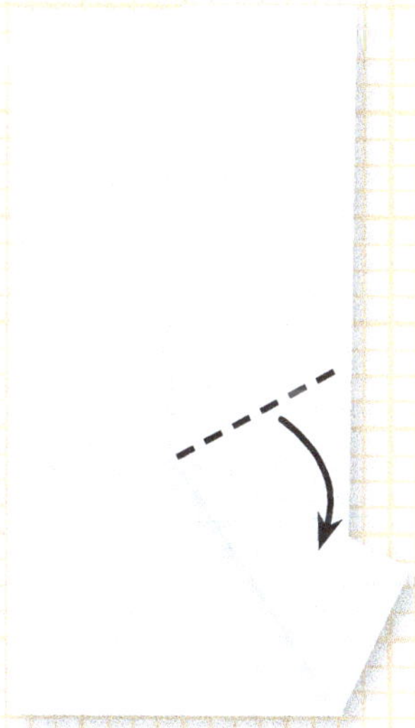

5

Take the bottom right corner and pull it up and to the side. Press down on the upper edge, as shown, to make a new crease.

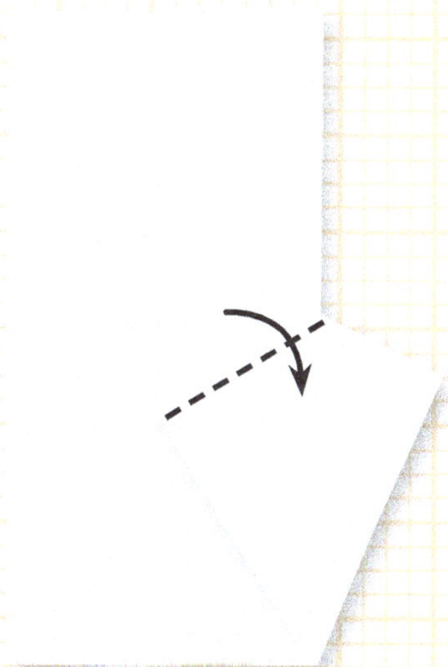

6 Flatten the paper to start off the thumb shape. Now fold down the corner as shown.

7 When you have this shape, open up the paper a little and pull down the corner slightly. Press flat to crease.

8 Mountain fold a ¾-inch (19 mm) strip at the bottom of the paper.

9 Fold the left edge in to meet the central crease.

10 Make a crease around 1½ inches (38 mm) from the top and fold the paper down.

11 Shape the thumb with valley folds along the right edges as shown.

12

Now fold in the tips of the top corners to shape the finger part of the glove.

13

Turn the paper over.

14

The right mitten is made.
To make the left mitten, follow the steps again, but make the creases and folds on the opposite side.

Beanie

A beanie is the perfect hat to keep your ears warm in cold weather. It's so simple to fold, you can make a different one for every day of the week.

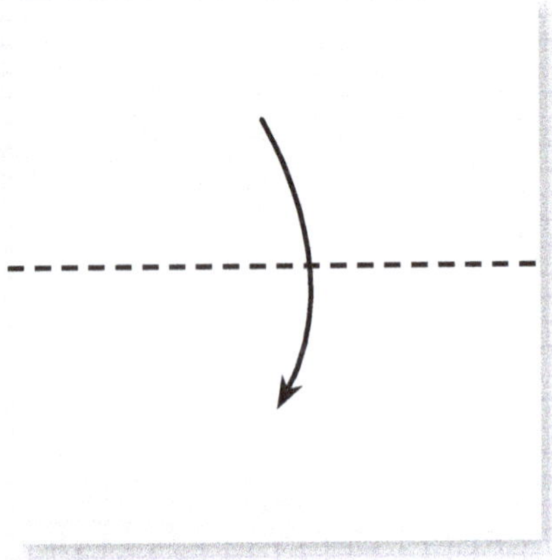

1 Fold the paper in half from top to bottom.

2 Make a crease in the left corner. Fold it over, making sure the edges are straight.

3 Fold over the right corner, making sure its bottom edge lines up with the one on the left.

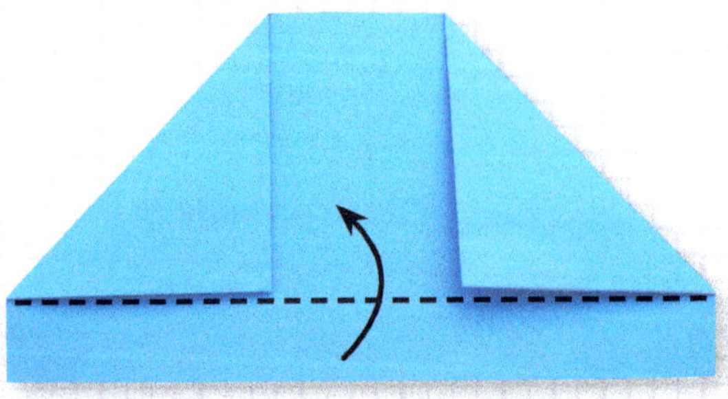

4 Now make the hat band. Taking the top layer, fold in the bottom edge just under the folded corners.

5 Now mountain fold the lower layer to complete the hat band.

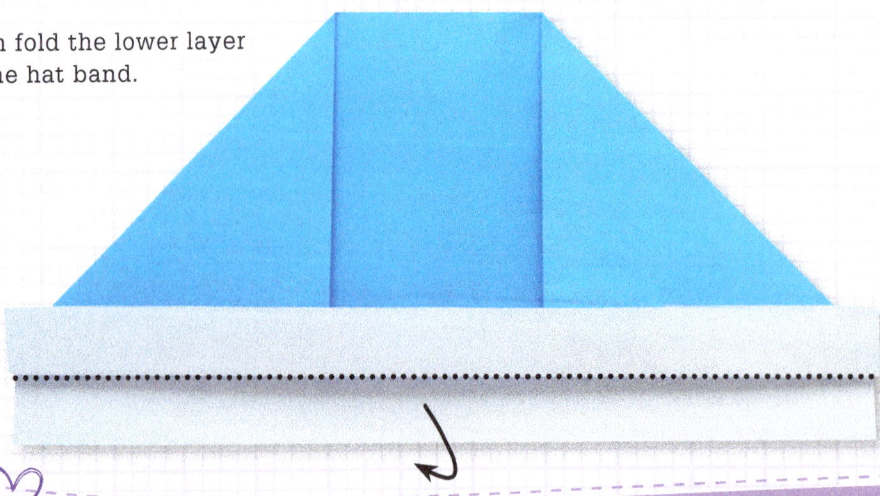

Easy

6 Fold in the left-hand point, as shown. Crease firmly.

7 Now fold in the right-hand point, creasing firmly once more.

8 Turn the paper over.

9 Your cozy, everyday beanie is complete. Add some snug mittens and you'll be ready for a wintry walk.

Crown

This fabulous crown is fit for a king or queen. Use yellow paper that glows like gold and it will sit proudly on any royal head.

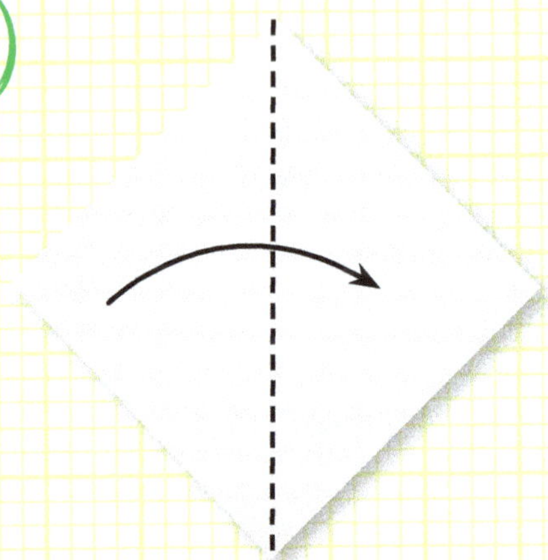

1 Place the paper as shown. Fold in half from left to right.

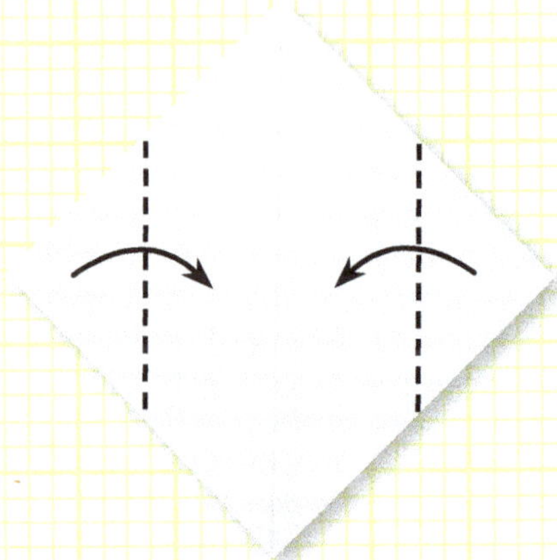

2 Fold in the left and right corners to meet the central crease.

3 Fold in the top and bottom corners in the same way.

4 You should now have a square. Turn the paper over.

5 Fold over the top edge to meet the central crease.

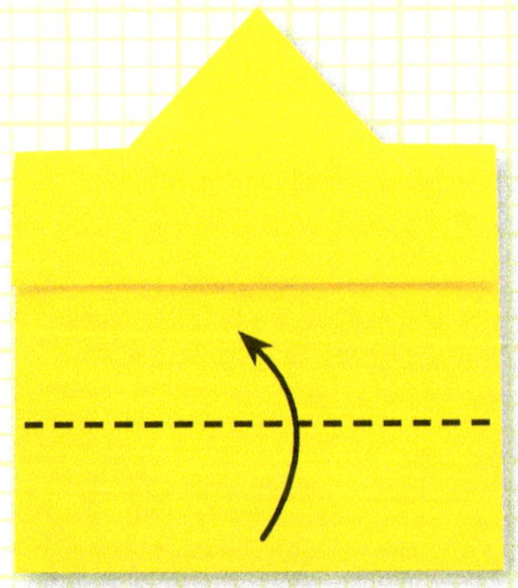

6 Repeat with the bottom edge.

7 Fold in the bottom triangle so the white side is showing.

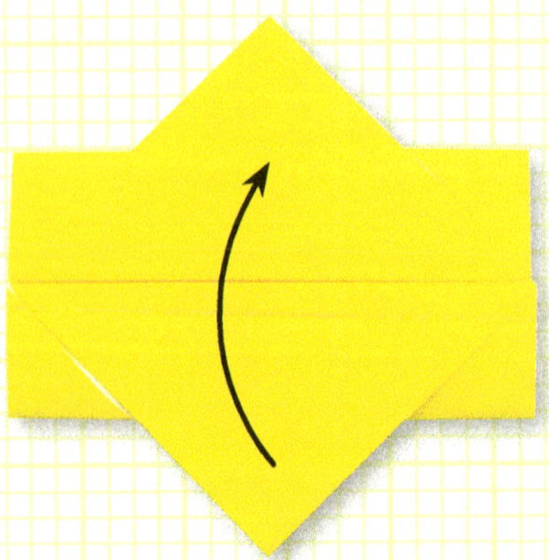

Easy

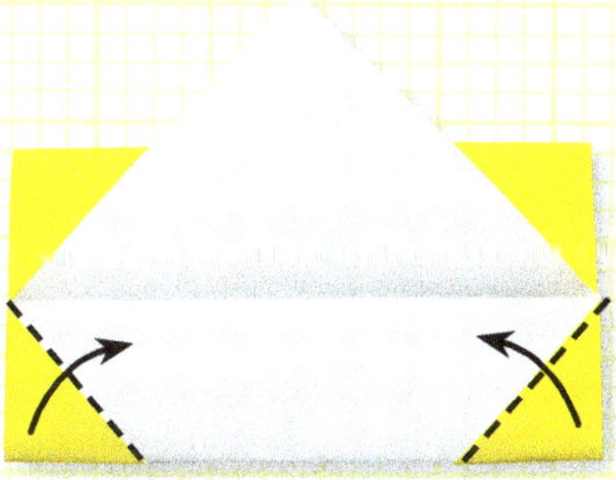

8 Valley fold the bottom corners to meet the central crease.

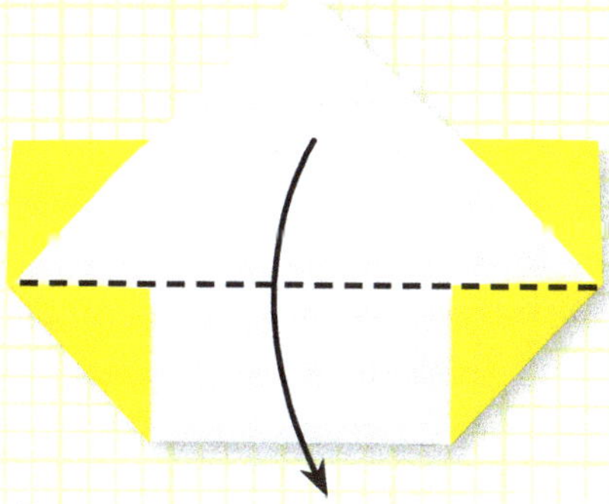

9 Fold down both layers of the triangle along the crease you made earlier.

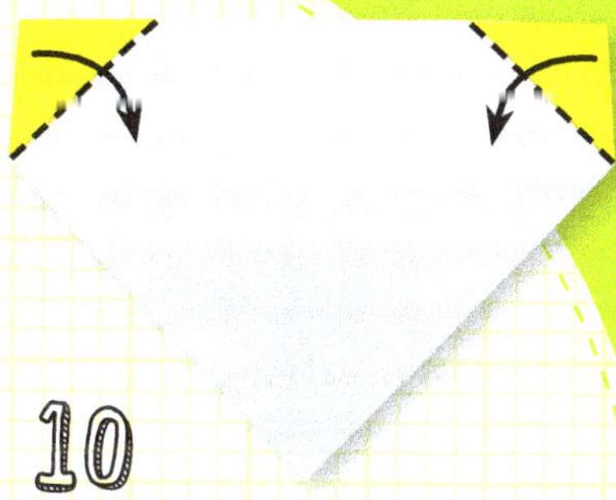

10 Now fold in the top corners to meet the central crease.

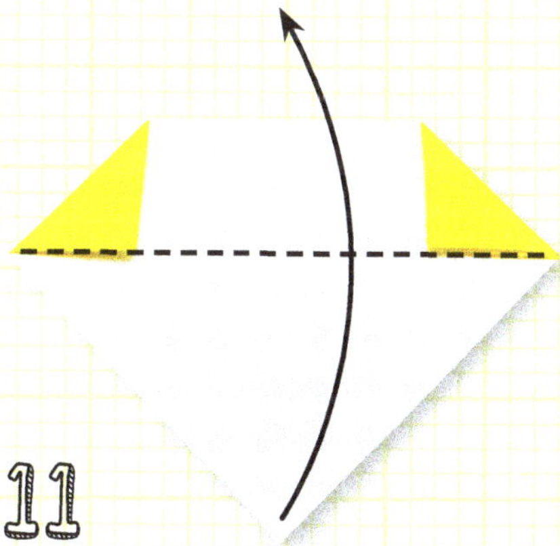

11 Fold over the top layer of the triangle to make a square.

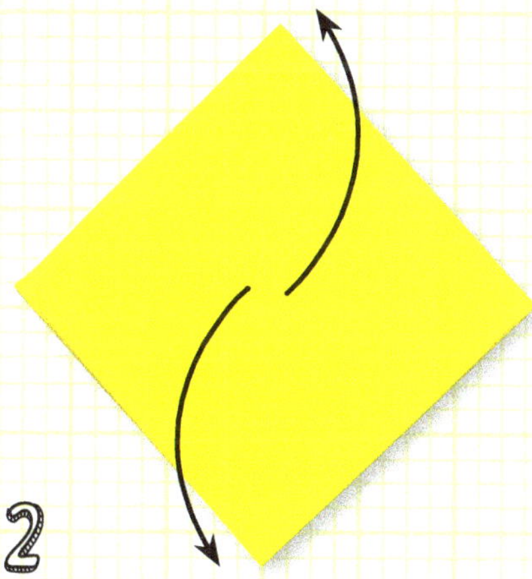

12 Hold the top and bottom corners and gently pull the triangles apart.

13 Pinch the creases between your fingers and work your way around the opening, making it round.

14 Turn your stately crown the right way up. Try adding some sparkling gem stickers for a totally regal look.

Wizard's Hat

Take a square of paper and conjure up a wizard's pointy hat. You don't need special powers, just a little paper-folding magic!

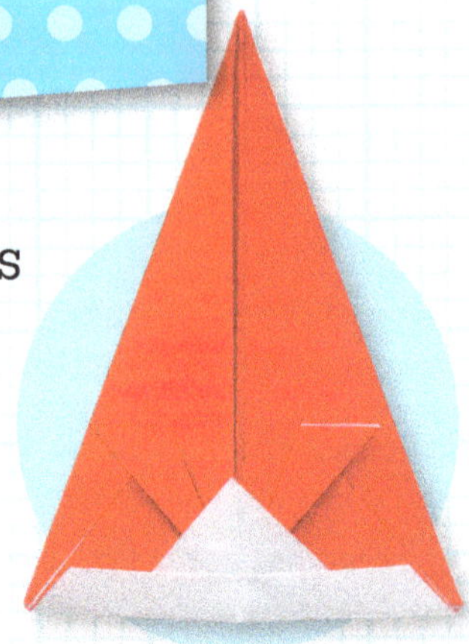

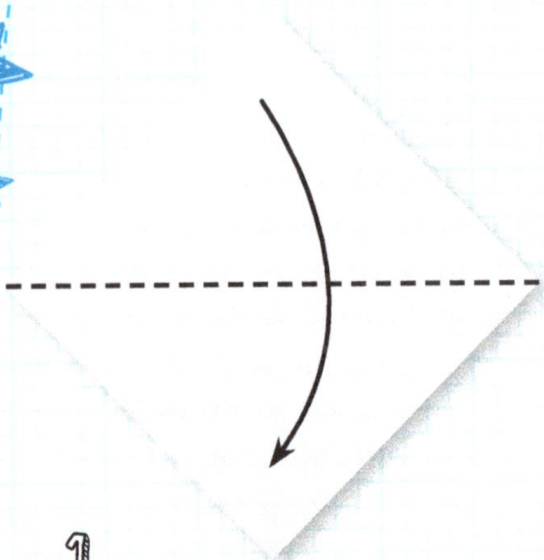

1

Place the paper as shown and fold it in half from top to bottom.

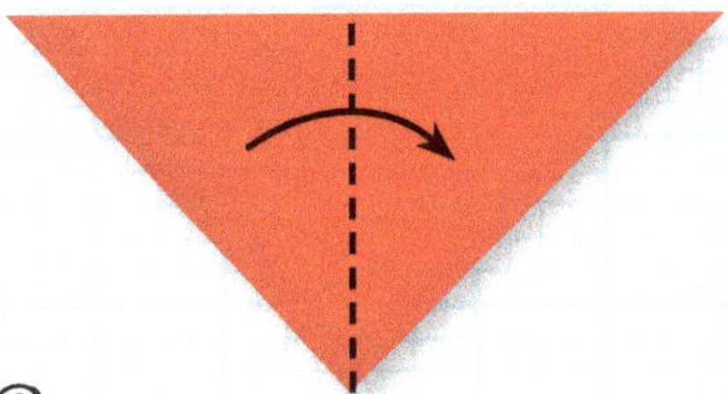

2

Fold it in half from left to right and unfold.

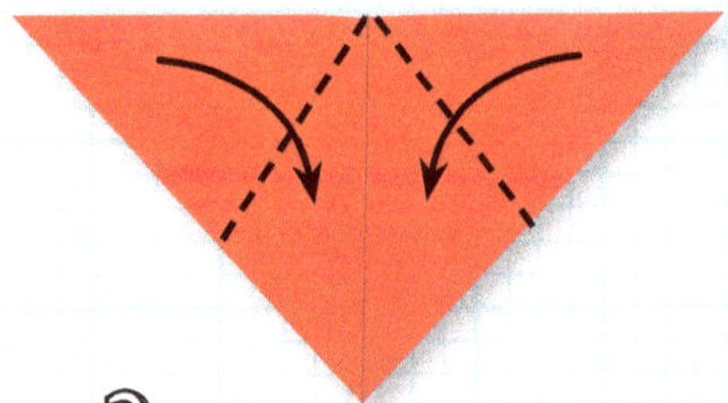

3

Fold in the top points to meet the bottom point. This makes a square.

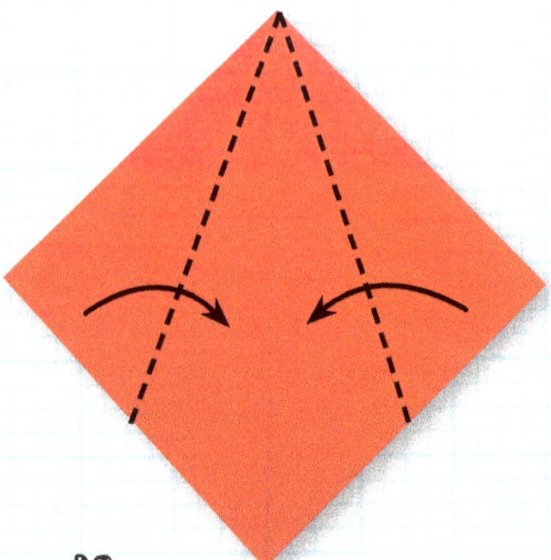

4

Fold in the left and right edges from the top corner to meet the central crease. This makes a kite shape.

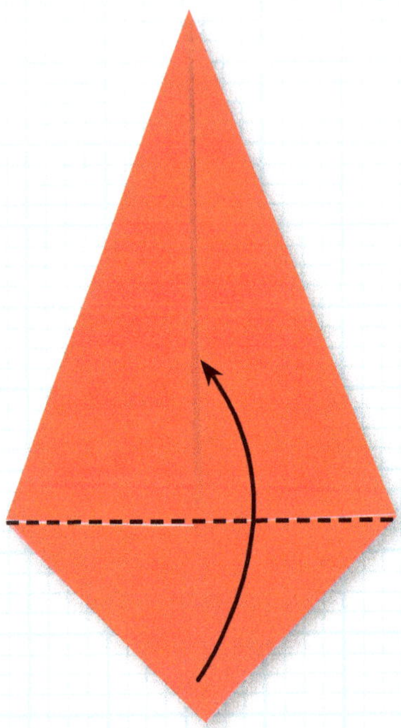

5 Taking the top layers only, fold in the bottom triangles.

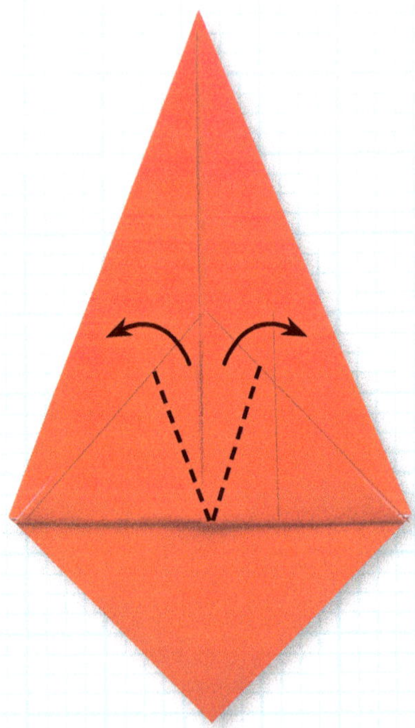

6 Make two angled creases that meet in a V. Fold the paper over so the points meet the outer edges.

Medium

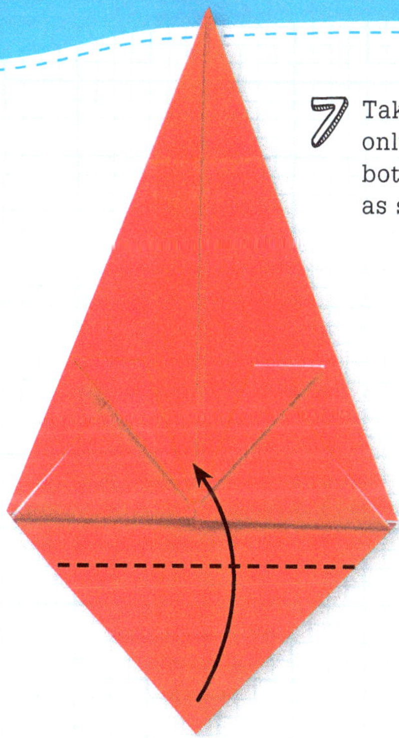

7 Taking the top layer only, fold in the bottom triangle as shown.

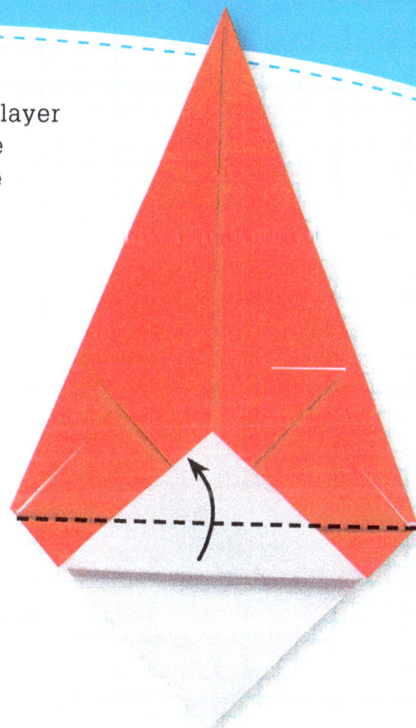

8 Fold in the top layer once more to line up with the bottom of the hat.

9 Take the remaining triangle and tuck it up inside the hat. Now open up the hat slightly so it stands up on its own.

10 Your hat is ready for some hocus-pocus! Draw on some stars and moons for extra pizzazz.

Pixie Hat

You could make some mischief with this enchanting pixie hat! Fold it carefully from forest green paper.

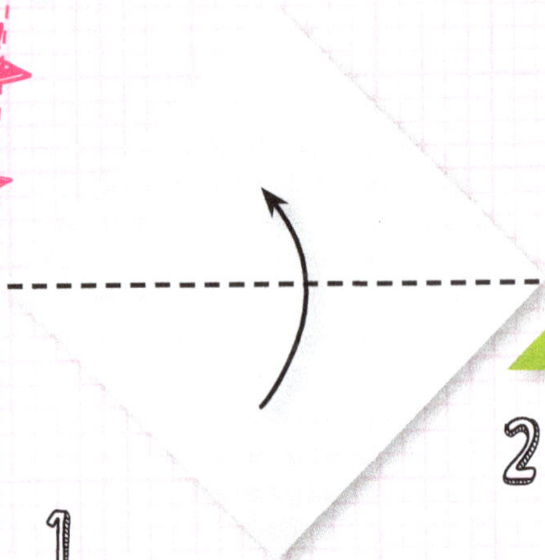

1 Place the paper as shown and fold it in half from bottom to top.

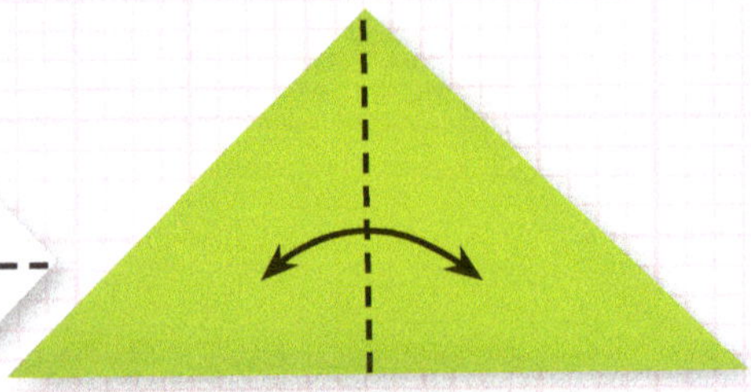

2 Fold the paper in half from left to right, then unfold.

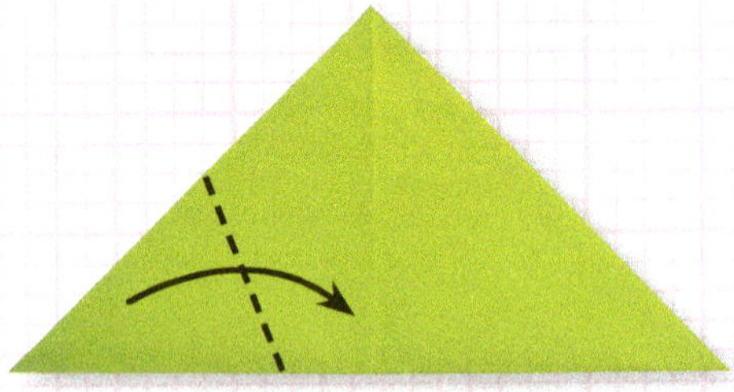

3 Fold over the left corner. The point should touch the right-hand edge and the top edge should be straight.

4 Repeat with the right corner. The top edges should overlap and line up.

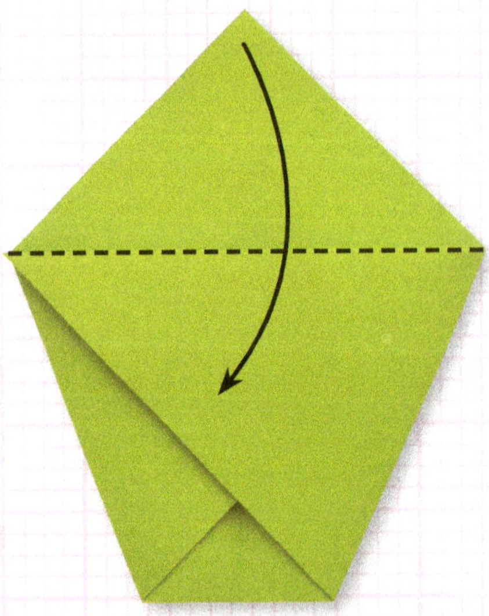

5 Make a crease just above the folded corners. Fold over the top layer of the top corner.

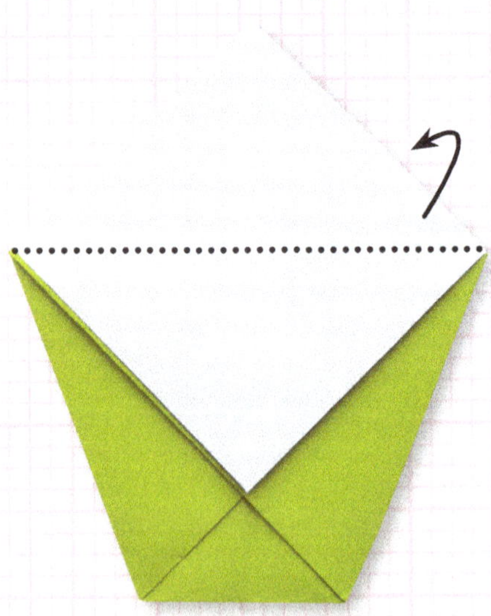

6 Mountain fold the bottom layer, as shown.

7 You now have a paper cup. Turn the cup upside down.

Medium

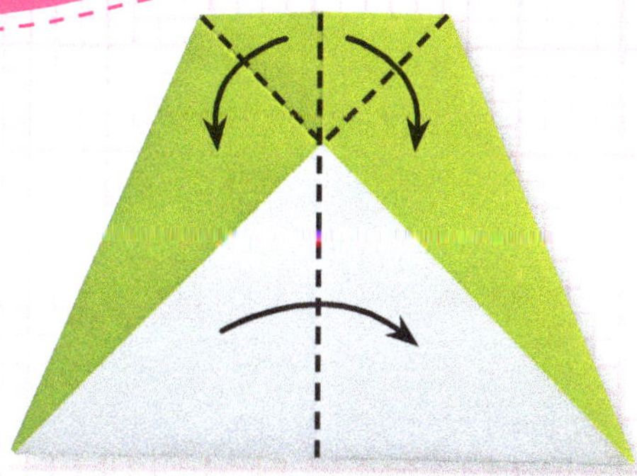

8 Crease along the edges of the triangle at the top. Now make a crease down the middle.

9 Fold the paper in half from left to right. Tuck in the triangle at the top as you fold to make the shape shown, then unfold again.

10

Make a crease around two-thirds of the way from the top of the white triangle and fold down.

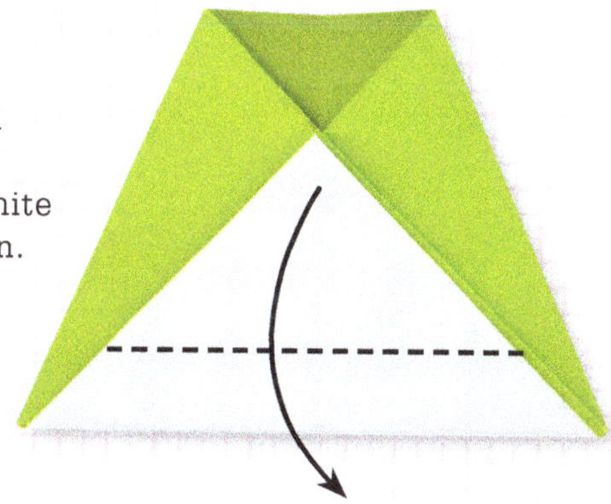

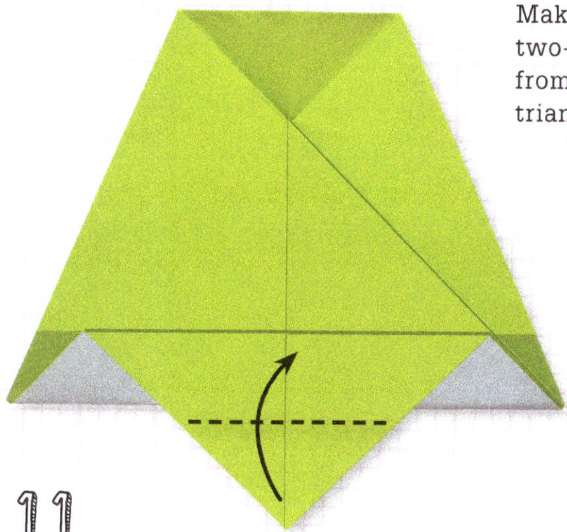

11

Fold the point back up so that the tip meets the edge of the fold you just made. This creates a zigzag pattern.

12

Open up the hat and press down on the top to make a dent. Your pixie hat is now ready to wear!

Cowboy Hat

No cowboy is complete without his hat. It keeps out the sun and the rain on long rides across the prairie, and it looks seriously cool!

1 Place the paper as shown and fold it in half from bottom to top.

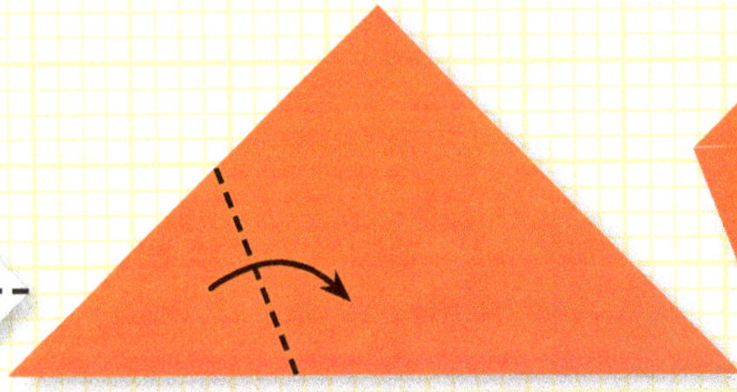

2 Fold over the left corner. The point should touch the right-hand edge and the top edge should be straight.

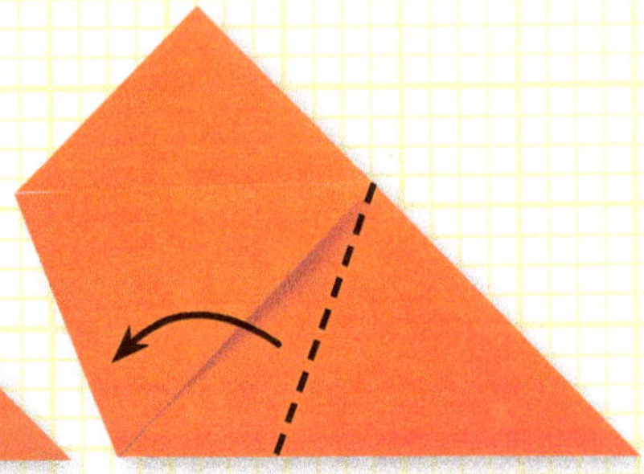

3 Repeat with the right corner. The top edges should overlap and line up.

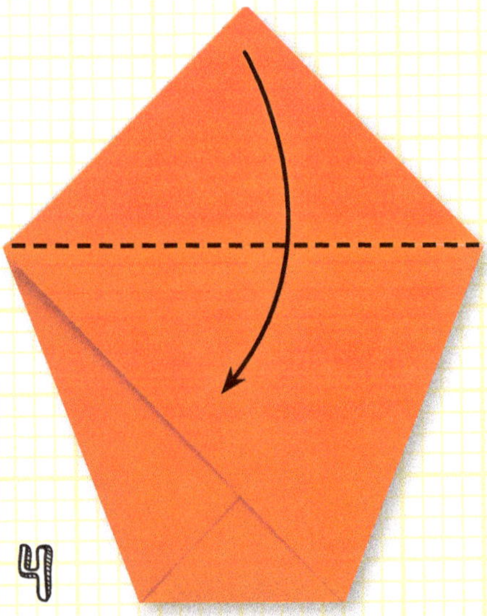

4 Make a crease just above the folded corners. Fold over the top layer of the top corner.

5 Mountain fold the bottom layer. You now have a paper cup!

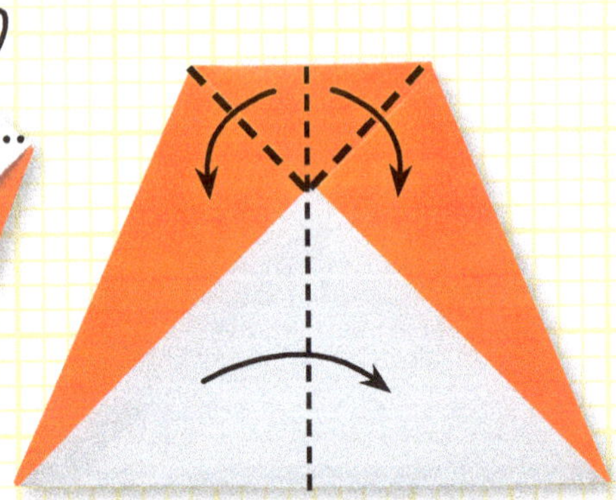

6 Turn the paper the other way up. Crease firmly along the edges of the triangle at the top, then fold the paper in half from left to right and unfold.

7 Open up the paper at the bottom, press down on the top, and push in the sides as shown.

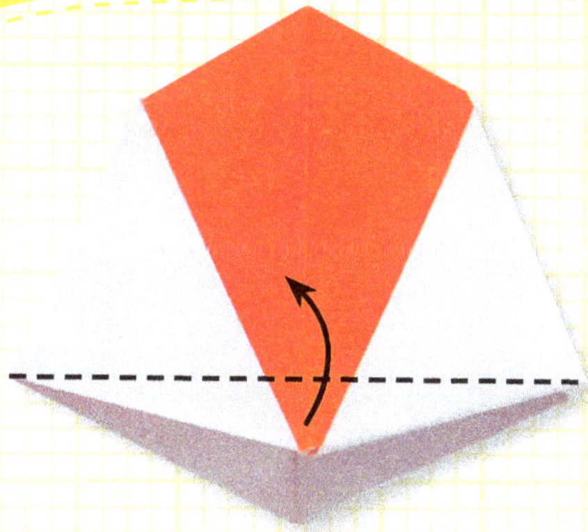

8 Your paper should look like this. Take the top layer of the bottom point and fold it up, as shown.

9 Now mountain fold the bottom layer.

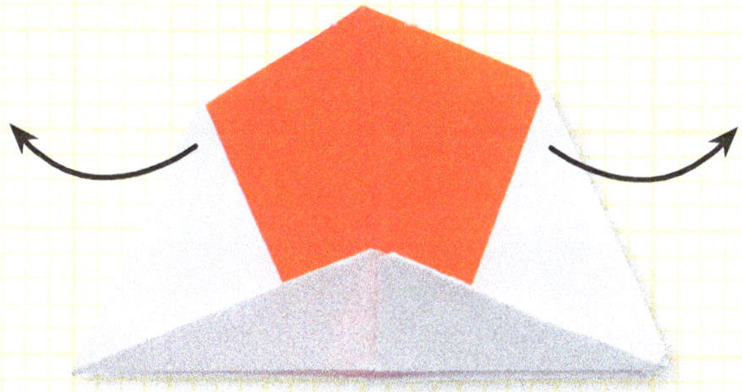

10 Gently pull down the white paper layer on either side. Flatten out the bottom edges.

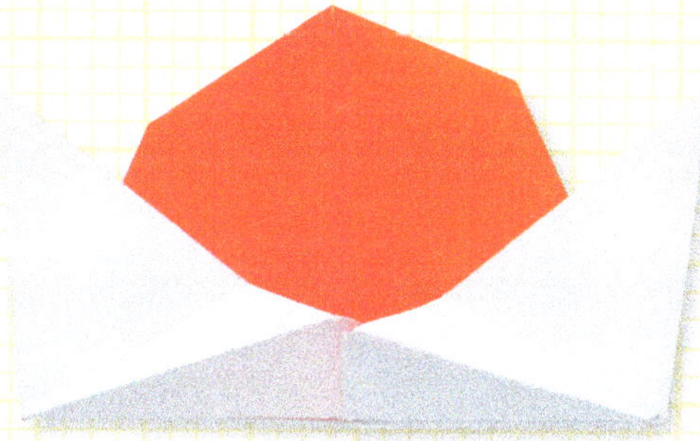

11 Open up the hat so it stands up on its own.

12 Your cowboy hat is ready to hit the trail. Saddle up your trusty horse and head off into the sunset!

Glossary

beanie A small, round, tight-fitting hat.

crease A line or mark made by folding something, such as a piece of paper. Also, to fold something so that a crease is formed.

garment Any item of clothing.

gem Precious stone, such as a diamond.

hocus-pocus Trickery.

pizzazz A quality that is exciting.

prairie Grassland.

regal To do with a king or queen.

shades Another word for sunglasses.

stately Elegant or majestic.

trim The edge of a piece of material.

Further Information

Books

George, Lauren Delaney. *L. Delaney's All Dolled Up: Creating a Paper Fashion Wardrobe for Paper Dolls*. Mineola, NY: Dover Publications, 2017.

Song, Sok. *Everyday Origami: A Foldable Fashion Guide*. North Mankato, MN: Capstone Press, 2016.

Song, Sok. *Origami Outfits: A Foldable Fashion Guide*. North Mankato, MN: Capstone Press, 2016.

Websites

en.origami-club.com/accessories/index.html
This website shows you how to make all kinds of origami accessories, from handbags and necklaces to umbrellas and sandals.

www.origami-instructions.com/origami-tote-bag.html
Follow the instructions on this page to make an origami tote bag.

Publisher's note to educators and parents: Our editors have carefully reviewed these websites to ensure that they are suitable for students. Many websites change frequently, however, and we cannot guarantee that a site's future contents will continue to meet our high standards of quality and educational value. Be advised that students should be closely supervised whenever they access the Internet.

Index